Mind Your Mouth

Sherry Elizabeth Brown

Phoenix Graphix Publishing Services, LLC.

Phoenix Graphix Publishing Services, LLC.
wendy@phoenixgraphix.us

Mind Your Mouth
Cover design by Belinda Seabright
Edited by Jana Cavalier and Wendy Hollinger

Printed in the United States
ISBN: 978-1-7346211-4-3
Library of Congress 2021912224

Contact Information:
Sherry Elizabeth Brown
www.motivationalmoments.org

Mind Your Mouth

What you say is first birthed in your mind then processed into your thoughts, and then they become spoken words which frame the world that you see and live in.

~ Sherry Elizabeth Brown

Dedication

This book is dedicated to my wonderful husband, who motivates, inspires, and fills my life with love and joy. I am honored to be your wife and to live this journey of blessings with you.

To my children, who continue to fill my life with joy and wonderful expectations for your future.

I am grateful to God for bringing us together as a family and for showing me that I am so very BLESSED.

Foreword

This book has been in the making for over 18 years. As most people, I thought that I had a plan. I knew that I would go through life just humming by like all the rest of the dreamers and goal setters of the time. As time started to march on and I was not seeing my life change—month after month, year after year—I started to seek and ask, "Ok, what gives here?" I am not a mean person. I am happy most of the time. I am a giver. I am an encourager, and I am upbeat and positive on a regular basis. I have a great husband, great kids, great family—so what gives? Why am I not seeing my goals, dreams and visions come to pass?

I was very frustrated with my perception of my life. I did not know why I was not seeing results.

As God is so awesome, kind and gentle, he started to take me on a journey and showed me that my problem was not my environment, not the house that I lived in, not the church that I attended, not the business associates that I have, not the people who are my friends, not even my career path. *The problem was approximately a half inch below my nose!*

Here's the thing: I am a get-it-done type of person. I do not like to wait. So, I have been heeding the Words in Habakkuk 2:2-3, which generally says to write the vision and make it plain [on paper] and to wait for it. Throughout this book, I am going to be very transparent with you as I take you through the journey that the Lord led me on. I am here to let you know the journey truly is worth the wait. I assure you, there is light at the end of this tunnel—not a train to run you over.

Thank you for picking up this book! I hope to inspire you and help you fulfill all that you believe God has placed in your heart and spirit for your life's journey.

As you read, feel free to skip around from chapter to chapter. I know that sometimes we need a go-to right away, so seek it out and use it for the given moment. I also know that sometimes when the storms of life hit, and Satan tries to make you think that you will be taken out of the battle, you now have a resource to fight that battle.

Use this as a guide to send Satan this message: "Not here, not now, not on my watch will you take from me all that God has promised to me and has in store for my future and my family!" (And it may help to say it aloud!)

Remember, you really are stronger than you think you are.

As you embark on this journey with me, I encourage you to journal in the margins, highlight and ponder what it is that God is speaking to you.

It is my prayer that you will find this to be encouraging—a way to look at things in a new perspective and to set you free from years of bondage that you may have not known you were entangled in.

I pray that you will also be comforted and empowered to become a better you—full of strength and resolve.

Let's get started setting you free by *Minding Your Mouth.*

Table of Contents

Chapter 1

Stop Speaking What You See

I am sure that I am not the only one who would say or think these statements: "My feelings will not determine how I walk by faith. My feelings are not holy. They are not solid. They will come and go. They are unpredictable and short-sighted." We are called to praise the Lord beyond what we see. We *should* say things like...

"When I feel that I have no strength, I will praise you. When I feel that I lack courage, I will praise you. When I have no bravery in me, I will praise you. When my mind tells me to fear, I will praise you. When I start to walk by sight and not faith, I will stop and change my direction. I will praise you."

This is not easy to do. It is much more difficult to do especially when you try to do it in your own strength and power, like I tried to do so many times without God guiding me. James hit the nail on the head when he said in James 3:8: "...no one can tame the tongue." (NASB) That is exactly what I was trying to do, all on my own. I thought, *really...it's just words? How hard can it be to say the right thing at the right time?* You know what I mean...when we are surrounded by people who love us, support us and are cheering us on, it is easy to say to yourself, *well, I am not like that guy getting mad in traffic; of course, I would not act or look like that.* Well guess what? Losing my cool is harder to control than I thought. So yes, I was taken to the mat, and I realized very fast, *yes, God, I do need help with my mouth!*

Having the ability to walk by faith and not by sight is so much easier said than done. We as people want to talk about everything! We want to interject our thoughts and our expertise into most things that come our way. At least we "think" we are the experts.

I started the book with the chapter title "Stop Speaking What You See" because I have walked for many years saying things I *saw* in the natural everyday life that I did not want to happen. I said that I was just stating the facts. I did not realize that I was receiving in my life what I had said yesterday. I had no idea that I was given the authority to call those things that I did not see into my reality. (See Romans 4:16-18) Yes, I have attended church my whole life and somehow, I missed this message. I thought, *Ok, if God can look at the darkness in Genesis and say, "let there be light," and it was so; and if I am truly an heir to Abraham, who is the father of many nations, then I should have this same authority and power, right?* This is where I started to really dig into what God meant from Genesis to Revelation about the power of what we say and what we do not say. I thought, *if this can help me, then maybe, just maybe, I am not alone in this way of thinking.*

I decided to look deeper into myself, who I had become, and where I was headed. Honestly, I did not like what I saw in the mirror. I especially did not like what was coming out of my mouth. Therefore, God led me to John 10:10. It became very clear once I really studied on this and what Jesus' intention for my life was and (in the very same verse) what Satan intended for my future. Jesus said in John 10:10 (ESV) that "the thief comes ONLY to steal and kill and destroy. I came that[you]may have life and have it abundantly." I thought, *Wow, how have I missed this?* This wraps it all up in one short verse—God's purpose and Satan's purpose. I realized I was on to something.

It took a very long time for me to guard my words like they were building my future to death or life. As a matter of fact, your words will become just that—death or life. What you say today will appear in one form or another tomorrow. That means it may take a day or two, or even years. I promise you it will show up in the future. The foundation of your words will be the foundation of your life. It starts with a thought, then an idea, then a word spoken (not thinking about it at all), and then it becomes a habit by saying it over and over. Finally, it seems to "just appear" out of nowhere in your life. It is no accident and no coincidence that it manifested in your life. You caused a chain reaction to it all. Did you catch that? You are the cause and reality of what you have. So that means that you are living today what you said yesterday. Here is the funny thing: most of us do not want to admit to this realization. I was one of those people. I did not want to admit that my life was not turning out as I wanted it to—based upon me and my words. I wanted to pass the blame (or the buck) on to someone else. I am sure that no one else does this...

I wanted to blame my home life, my finances, my family who lived in my house, my extended family—anyone but me. Here is the truth of the matter: it is based upon me! I am the only one who will do my pushups for me. Meaning, I am the only one who can reshape my life if I want to. If I don't want to, then that is my choice, but then I have no right to pass that on to someone else. You see, I have learned this the hard way. As an independent business owner in the direct sales arena, anyone knows that if I do not "mind my mind," it will flow downhill. This is not only true in a business sense, but also on the home front.

God gave women a special place. What we exhibit in the home or in our emotions, will flow all throughout the house. We have all heard, that "if Momma is not happy, no one is happy." I do believe that there is great truth in this.

I have been so blessed to be the mother of two wonderful children who are now young adults, so I learned this many years ago when I was just learning how to be a mom. When I heard other moms talk about their toddlers and how "little devils" or "little witches" they were, I was shocked that they would say something like that to that beautiful little child. They would say, "Oh, but you don't live with them." Well, who would want to live with devils and witches—no thank you!

I would like to think at the time that my two kids were "angels," however, they were normal kids who wanted to see what their boundaries were. Not that this is a book about how to raise children, but I think it is important to mention that as a parent, if you do not set boundaries, and if your children do not know what is acceptable in the home and what is not, that can cause more trial and error in years to come. Many situations can be avoided if just handled right, mainly by how we speak about the situation.

We did a lot of teaching and training when they were younger. We would not call toddler phases the "terrible twos"; it was the "terrific twos." Likewise, we did not call it the "trying threes"; it was the "discovering new territory threes." The teaching and training were all in how we addressed situations. For example, if they were old enough to pull all the plastic containers out of the cabinet to play hide and seek, then they were old enough to clean up and put them all back. This required extra patience and praise on our part to instill this in them in the early years.

I did my best to say "yes" to them more than I said "no" on a single day… "Yes, you can play in the sand. Yes, you can unload the plastic container cabinet and build a fort. Yes, you can play hide-and-seek in the bottom of the closet. Yes, you can set up your army men and make a fort out of the whole kitchen floor." Unlike, "No, you cannot spray paint the dog. No, you cannot cut your sister's hair. No, you cannot use that knife to dig in the dirt; let's use a shovel instead." It all had to do with what my husband and I would say over them. Also, at the time, I did not realize the impact that it would make on my life in the years to come. It was simple, quick decisions that we had to make in that moment. I am blessed and honored to say that we now have two amazing young adults, and I am very humbled that they have turned out to be great.

So now as I look back on all that time and training that we did, many times falling into bed exhausted and asking God, "Was I too harsh? Did I ruin them for the rest of their lives?" Here is the good news that God shared with me on those days many years ago and even today.

He told me that today is a new day, old things, old sayings, old ways of doing things have passed away—meaning it is gone. I can reset my life and the outcome, regardless of my age or my past experiences. Wow, that will set you free if you allow your mind to wrap around that for a moment.

This valuable lesson that I learned was that there is a way to change your future simply by changing your words. Start today. If it is negative, don't say it; if it does not lift or build up, put your hand over your mouth and don't give life to it. Do not allow that to hit the atmosphere. You see, when you do not say it—even if you think it—the words do not cross over the threshold of your mouth. It is like fruit dying on the vine; you have cut off all flow of life to it. You have taken charge over your destiny for tomorrow. You have taken control. You are the one in charge—not your mind, not your mouth. Your spirit will rise, and you will start to build and grow in your confidence and your love for yourself. I realized that I could not do it without the power of God flowing through me and showing me His amazing grace to help me with my mind and my mouth daily.

You see part of what I had to learn in the journey of this process was that I had to start to learn to love myself for who I am and how God made me.

I had to realize that only God knows the thoughts and the intentions of my heart. Satan cannot read my mind. He only sees what my reactions and attitudes are and what may come out of my mouth in reference to a situation. Then he says, "OK, let's see how I can mess her up with what she said and cause her confusion."

But what we need to do is throw confusion into the enemy's camp. Often times you know that a mind trap is being set for you—the bills are due, the water does not work, the baby or the dog just threw up on the floor, the dishes are overflowing, the laundry is starting to spring legs of its own and walk into another room...I could go on and on. You see the picture. It can feel like a position of lack, quickly being overwhelmed and hopeless. However, by addressing these situations that come to us daily, we can speak words of life and praise, saying,

"Lord, I praise you! You said that you will supply all my needs according to your riches in glory." (See Phil. 4:19) "Lord, thank you that you are turning this overwhelming situation around for your glory and my good." That is when you throw confusion into his camp—you give him no power to control you.

You can set yourself free with praise. This is how it may sound like:

"God, I praise you that I have a laundry full of dirty clothes and a kitchen full of dirty dishes. That means my family is healthy and active. Thank you, God, for all this activity. God, I praise you that I have bills to pay, that means we are prospering, and we have electric, water, a home, and a car. Thank you, God, that I have the privilege and the honor to pay the bills. That means I can see you perform a miracle."

Do you see how this can really cause chaos in the kingdom of hell? The devil and his demons will be like, *What are they doing? They are praising God for that situation.* In this way, you gave him no power to mess with your life. You equipped yourself with the Word of God for that day, and you instantly saw the trap; and because you were equipped, you did not fall into the trap.

Here is something else that I am learning—to this day and each day: I need to reset my mind, reset my attitude every day. I cannot live off yesterday's blessings. God has new ones for me today. So even as I am getting out of bed and looking to start my day, the FIRST words of the day are VERY, VERY important. Let your praise set the tone of your day. "God, I praise you for this beautiful day." (It may be raining, snowing, or storming!) You are setting the stage for your production of the day to begin. "God, I thank you that I will be able to handle all that you have in store for me this day; you have equipped me and given me strength to handle what I may encounter." I expect something good to happen to me and through me today to honor your kingdom.

One morning I had woken up and found that our new English bull dogs that we just bought had thrown up again during the night and messed in their cages. This was the fifth morning in a row that this had happened! I was done! When I am running the steam vac at 6:30 a.m. even before the kids are up, before coffee or tea, something had to give. I thought, *OK God, I can handle only so much, either we need to find a new home for these dogs, or I need a new home with a facility name across the front of the building.* Obviously, I am still here, and we did find good homes for the dogs. God does have a sense of humor!

Here is something to think about: Satan is not creative at all; he is smart, and he is a fallen angel, but he is not creative. Think about it: there are basically only three areas of your life that he tries to mess with.

* Your health

* Your finances

* Your relationships

I know that may sound simple but think about it. Break it down. All that you deal with in life can be broken down into one of these categories: your health or a family member or friend's health; your finances, personal or business; or your relationships—whether they be in the home, at work or even in the church.

We sometimes get "pigeon-holed" as to who we are and who our identity becomes. We become a stay-at-home mom, and we feel that is all the value we have. We become the secretary at the office who only makes copies, answers the phone, and greets people. That is all the value that we feel we have because we have done it for such a long time. We believe that we are that student who is always in school, at school, studying and studying more...will we ever arrive at our destiny? We are that husband, that father who goes to workday in and day out to provide for our family's needs. We hate our jobs, we dislike our bosses, but we take the ticket that has been sold to us because we believe that this is all the potential that we have inside of us.

But we are created with so much more inside of us that we could possibly be imagine. Don't let yourself fall into one of Satan's traps that I mentioned earlier. Remember, he tries to make you think that you are only of value in one area and no other. Be bold, study the Word, and you will truly find out who you are. You are a child of the highest king. If you are a stay-at-home mom, work in an office, or clean houses for a living, whatever it may be, be the best that you can be at it and realize the tactics that Satan will use to try to keep you "stuck" in your thinking.

I was recently reading *The Prayer of Jabez* by Bruce Wilkerson, and in the book he tells a story of a man who goes to Heaven and sees this amazing, beautiful, magnificent building; and when he inquires what it is, Peter says to him, "You do not want to go in there and see that." So, the man thought, *this is Heaven, there are no secrets in Heaven.* So, he runs to the building, flings open wide the door, and sees these beautiful shelves from floor to ceiling with white boxes and glorious red ribbons on each box. He turns to Peter and asks, "Do I have a box?" He then took off running to find his name alphabetically on the shelves. With great glee and delight he finds his box and even before he opens the lid

Peter braces himself for the same reaction as the many who have come before him. A great disappointed sigh fills the rows of untapped blessings, unused gifts that were placed inside of the man that he did not believe he could achieve while on earth.

This really hit me hard when I came across this. It made me stop reading and quickly and instantly repent. And I asked this question to God in a whisper, "What have I missed out on because of fear? Because of unbelief? Because of doubt? Because I did not see myself as being good enough?"

As I stated earlier, in the process of this journey, I have had to learn how to love myself for who I am and who God created me to be—not what I thought of myself.

Chapter 2

Reshape Your Life

Thoughts, emotions, and feelings are very fickle. They will lead you astray each time if you decide to give into them. They have no foundation and no proof of the future God has in store for you. They are not based on fact. They are based on what-ifs.

All our decisions and actions come about simply by one thought. It has been said that the average person thinks between 15,000 and 60,000 thoughts per day. Meditating on the sheer number of that is very overwhelming. For those of us on the high end of that number, your mind may function like this: *Do I go to the grocery store first or the library? When should I start the laundry? If I do it now, then I can change the beds at the same time then I can go clean up take a shower and then go to the grocery store then the library. Well, no if I do that then the dishes will need to be put away and I must go to the school and pick up the kids, but if I leave early and not get stuck in traffic, I can make that work. Oh, wow my hair and face are really a mess.* (I caught a glimpse of myself as I was leaning over to pick up the trash and start to run the vacuum.) *Now that I am in the bathroom, quick, I can Windex down the mirror. Oh no, that is not a good look, I need to get a wax done. When will I have time to fit that in? Oh, I can do it myself and well no that won't work I got wax all over the counter last time I tried that, and my husband was not happy. Oh, I can see my roots, need to schedule a hair appointment. Oh, look at the time, I need to get the kids from school, take a shower and go to the store. Now I don't have time for a shower, so where is my ball cap and sweatshirt? I am not pretty. It will not matter. Why do I need to feel good about myself? Why would I need to feel of value? I am just a mom; I am just a wife. No big deal. Now I am exhausted. Where did my day go? I did not get to work out. What does it matter? Gravity is taking over—I may as well assist it. Where is that ice cream? Ugh, now the freeze door was left open! Who did this? Now I need to clean out the freezer. Why would it matter anyway? No one appreciates all that I do around here!*

So… with this funny little example, you see all the things that can literally run the superhighway of your thought life. Perhaps we have all experienced something like this. But what we need to do is think on purpose. Yes, that is right. Make your thinking purposeful thinking. With 15,000–60,000 thoughts and 70–80% on average are toxic and negative, it is no wonder we have so many people feeling like they are defeated even before they get out of bed. No wonder we have so many depressed, overweight, unhealthy, unhappy people in our society. They have given up on themselves. You can see how powerful your thoughts are and how they can frame your life. Our most dominate thoughts will take us in the direction that our lives will go.

Here is the sad truth to all of this: It all started with a simple thought. If it started with a simple thought, then it can be changed with a simple thought, right? Yes, it can! Can you hear me screaming from the roof tops? Well, I am really just sitting on the floor in my living room with my laptop! But you get the idea of how much I want you to grab hold of this concept. If you say to yourself, "I am worthy, I am pretty, God made me, I have a purpose, I am of great value, I am a child of the highest king." Then what will happen, when you think it, you will begin to believe it. You really can change the direction of your future by what you think. Then you must speak it out.

Did you know that the primary purpose of words is to release creative power not merely communication?

That power could sound something like this: "There is joy in my mouth because of your word, oh God. There is financial peace and security in your word. I speak to the mountain." I praise the Lord first, then the mountain will move. This is based upon Mark 11: 22-24 (MSG);

"Embrace this God-life. Really embrace it, and nothing will be too much for you. This mountain, for instance: Just say," Go jump in the lake"—no shuffling or shill-shallying—and it's as good as done. That's why I urge you to pray for absolutely everything, ranging from small to large. Include everything as you embrace this God-life, and you'll get God's everything."

Praise is recorded in the Bible 248 times. Oftentimes, my praise sounds like this: "I will cry out to you with praises in my heart and on my lips. I will surround myself with your word daily. I will read it. I will speak your word. I will teach and train it to all who are around me. I will walk in your word. I will do your word daily. I will praise you. I will have hope in you. I will live in you. I will be confident in you. I will meditate on your goodness. I will be refreshed by your word. I will be renewed by your word."

Praise. Praise. Praise.

Romans 12:2 (paraphrased) is a great reference for this: Let God transform you into a new person by changing the way you think.

Chapter 3

Speak the Word Only

Psalm 103:20-21; "So bless God, you angels, ready and able to fly at his bidding, quick to hear and do what he says. Bless God, all you armies of angels, alert to respond to whatever he wills."

I became very excited when I was studying out this scripture several years ago. It made me think of the Kentucky Derby. The horses that run this prestigious 1.25-mile event are trained to run and to race. It is in their blood. It is what they are bred for. They are not to pull carts or buggies. They are not to work in the fields pulling plows. They are bred to race—that is it.

As I was going over and over this scripture, another picture God shared with me was this: The angels are waiting for us—God's sons and daughters—to speak the Word only. The angels are at our beck and call to fulfill what the Word of God has in store for us. We are to be the ambassadors to speak the Word in the land, to be able to speak out the calling that we have on our lives. But here is the great wonder of God's mercy and grace that he extends to us all. Can you see the picture: we spend time with the Lord in prayer, we speak the Word, we pray the Word, and we believe all that it says about us and our lives and any situations that we are currently in. We set the angels out to "heed the voice in the land,"—that is your voice speaking the Word of God over your situation. Then you decide to "call" a friend and you start to speak your fears, your doubts and even unbelief over what had just been set in motion with the angels heeding the Word. Now they are coming to a screeching halt because you released the words of doubt in the land. Can you see what I am talking about and why it is so very important to know the power of what you are speaking?

This is what he was showing me about "heeding the Word." We are to speak to our mountain about how great our God is, not how big our mountain is to God. Mark 11:22-24 tells us that, "... have faith in God. Some translations say, have the faith of God. The God kind of faith. For assuredly, I say to you, whoever says to this mountain, 'Be removed and be cast into the sea,' and does not doubt in his heart, but believes that those things he says will be done, he will have whatever he says. Therefore, I say to you, whatever things you ask when you pray, believe that you receive them, and you will have them."

Do you see the correlation to all of this? We really do have to be very aware of what we are saying when we have finished saying the amen and are waiting for the answer to show up. This is a space of time that I was not aware of before God showed this to me in his Word. I was like most people. I would pray, believe that it would happen and then just wait for it to show up. Not giving it a second thought. If it never came to pass, I must've had something to do with it. I just thought, oh well, God did not hear my prayers, or he did not want me to have that, or you know something must have caught his attention and he had more important things to do.

All that negative thinking is not right or from the kingdom of God. It is from the pit of hell, which I had been listening to for so many years. I finally got the revelation that God was showing me—that I do have a part to play in this as well. My goodness, wow, that really got my attention! I thought, *really…I have something to do with this? I need to be more aware of my words? You mean that I can set the course of my future and each day based upon my words?* Thank you, God, for me finally getting this to sink through my thick skull!

Faith is not what we see or feel, it is what we believe to be God's word and the right word. God will not become upset with me when I ask him what I can imagine having it become a reality. God is not upset or unhappy with me. He has designed me to ask big dreams, to have big visions and to become all that he wants me to be.

Chapter 4

Sarcasm vs. Kindness

When we think of kindness, most people think of it as toward others. That is true and important. However, I want to address kindness to yourself. Many times, we will speak to ourselves cruel and unkind words that we would never utter to anyone else. I want to help you change what you think and say about yourself on a daily basis. We are to speak words of healing, life, faith and hope over ourselves anything else, keep quiet. Do not say a thing. Romans 10:10 (NKJV) says, "For with the heart one believes unto righteousness, and with the mouth confession is made unto salvation." Mark 11:23 says, "For assuredly [with total confidence], I say to you, whosoever says to this mountain, 'Be removed and be cast into the sea,' and does not doubt in his heart, but believes that those things he says will be done, he will have whatever he says."

there is so much "meat" here in this scripture to digest. First off, what are some mountains in your life right now? Sickness? Lack? A pile of bills? Relationships on the rocks? Your family members not serving the Lord the way they should? Pressure on the job? What does your mountain that you are facing currently look like?

Speak to that mountain and tell it how big your God is—don't tell God how big your mountain is. He already knows. One of my favorite scriptures is Psalm 103:20-22: "Bless the Lord, you His angels, Who excel in strength, who do His word, Heeding the voice of His word. Bless the Lord, all you His hosts, you ministers of His, who do His pleasure. Bless the Lord, all His works, in all places of His dominion. Bless the Lord, O my soul!" (NKJV) Do you understand the authority that has been given to us in this set of scriptures? When we speak the Word of the Lord, the angel armies are at our beck and call. Wow! Also, in Hebrews 1:14 they are called ministering angels to assist us in this life. Wrap your head around that one. Why are we living below what God has designed for us? Could it be based upon the words that we do or do not speak? Could it be that what we are projecting into the atmosphere the cause and effect of what we receive?

One last scripture to give additional understanding to the part we play in implementing all that occurs in our lives. Hebrews 11:6 says, "But without faith it is impossible to please Him, for he who comes to God must believe that He is, and that He is a rewarder of those who diligently seek Him." (NKJV) YES! You have a part in this. It is a faith journey, each day. Our faith is renewed daily. As we stand in faith, believing that what the Word says about us is true regardless if we feel like it or not.

I titled this chapter sarcasm vs. kindness. Let's take some time and talk about sarcasm. I guess that I did not realize how prevalent it has become in our society. However, the more I studied this out, it is not limited to any generation. Remember that Satan is no respecter of persons. He does not care who you are, where you have come from or even where you are planning on going. He does not care about your goals, visions, or dreams in the slightest. He wants to stop you. He has one plan and only one plan for your life and that is to kill, steal and destroy. Jesus said that he came to give life and for us to have it abundantly. (See John 10:10.) Where does the sarcasm come from? Before we answer that, what is the definition of sarcasm? According to Merriam-Webster, a sharp and often satirical or ironic utterance designed to cut or give pain.

It is a remark made usually to hurt someone's feelings or show scorn. The actual root of sarcasm comes from a Greek verb, *sarkazein*, which means "to tear flesh like a dog." It also carries the meaning of "to bite one's lip in rage," "to gnash one's teeth," and lastly, "to sneer." So now you can see that sarcasm can be sharp, cutting or wounding.

Here is the question, is sarcasm sin? Can we sin with our mouths/words? I believe that we all have been affected by sarcasm in one way or another. I believe that our society has made a joke about it. We see it everywhere, all over social media, with our family and friends. It is even throughout our churches. We laugh it off, say it is funny. Or "I was just giving you a hard time." If the Word of God says to guard our mouths even in jesting, would that also include sarcasm? Is a little of it OK? Not intending to hurt someone's feelings but we should let them know we are not comfortable with what they say or do. We cut with our words. Is it really our job? Do we really want that rod of judgment to extend over others? (Warning: It will be extended back over us!)

When we think of sarcasm, here is a biblically example, maybe we think of how a husband and wife may speak to each other. Michal, David's wife in 2 Samuel 6:20 (MSG), said to him, when he was seen dancing in the streets to glorify God after a victory, "How wonderfully the king has distinguished himself today exposing himself to the eyes of the servants' maids like some burlesque street dancer!" Wow! I am sure that was not the greeting that David was expecting after a hard-fought battle for the kingdom. If Michal was embarrassed by David's actions, why did she not realize that he was not concerned with what she thought of him, but what God thought of him? She could have said something like, "Sweetie, I really appreciate that you are not hindered by what others think of you. You are the king, so you have set the bar high of how to praise God." But the interesting thing is how David responded back to her in the next verse: "In God's presence I'll dance all I want! He chose me over your father and the rest of our family and made me prince over God's people, over Israel. Oh yes, I'll dance to God's glory, more recklessly even than this. As far as I'm concerned, I'll gladly look like a fool… but among these maids you're so worried about, I'll be honored no end." (2 Samuel 6:21 MSG)

As we dig deeper into this subject of sarcasm, I think it really boils down to what other people will think. So maybe to guard or protect yourself you will use sarcasm to cover or hide your own feelings of self-worth.

Then to top it all off, guess what happened to Michal? From that time forward, she was barren for the rest of her life. Wow, again, the power of our words can change our future. If Michal's intent was to hurt David because she was embarrassed, then it is true that what you sow you will reap. She wanted him to stop praising God. He had just brought victory and life to the kingdom of Israel. But what she wanted him to do was stop rejoicing over the life and abundance that was brought into the kingdom, and she got just that. No life would be produced from her body ever again.

Chapter 5

Speaking Perverse Words

Many times, when you hear the word *perverse* or *deceitful* you may think, well that means swearing, curse words or even lying, right? That is what I thought until I decided to really dig into it and find out what God meant when he said, "Put away from you a deceitful mouth, and put perverse lips far from you." (Proverbs 4:24 NKJV)

Webster's definition of *perverse*: morally bad, corrupt, stubborn in opposing what is right, reasonable, or accepted, irritable, cranky, perverted. Also, Webster's definition of *deceitful*: practicing or tending to practice trickery, showing, or containing deceit or fraud.

This is not at all what I thought it would be. When we break it down, we may not really like what we find out when we explore this scripture.

When you think of something that would be corrupt, it would not be pure or clean or whole. So therefore, it is a perversion of God's word for our lives.

When you speak opposite of the truth of God, again, you are speaking perverse words (e.g., "God never hears me when I pray. Why has God not answered my prayers, yet he must not love me. Well, God must love 'sister so and so more' than he loves me.") All these statements do not line up with God's word. Therefore, you are releasing perverse words over your life.

Have you ever been irritable, cranky, or stubborn with your words? Have you ever determined that you are right no matter what, and you will drive your point or attitude home, regardless of how the other person may think about the situation?

I am sure I am not the only one who has done this—in the heat of the moment, you are so determined to offer a piece of your mind that you get so far off track, and before you know it, you start to say things that you would not normally let fly out of your mouth. You think, *Oh my! How did we get here?* and Wow, *I can't believe that I just said that out loud!*

When you speak perverse or deceitful words it can result in a three-fold return in your life.

1. Lack, poverty, Sickness, disease (or dis-ease)
2. Unhealthy relationships
3. Spiritual death

1. Let's look deeper at each area, lack, poverty, sickness, disease (or dis-ease)

God did not place lack or poverty on you to teach you a lesson or to get you to honor and serve him. If that were the case, then God is a bully, and he is not a loving God whom I want to serve.

Think about this: Of all the people who came to Jesus in the Bible to be healed, whether mentally, physically, or financially, how many went away not healed, restored, or provided for? Not a one of them. He healed and restored each one of them. So why do we think that sickness and disease are from the kingdom of God? Should we really believe that these problems are trying to teach us something? No. That is a lie from the pit of hell! This goes back to what I said in the beginning; you need to know that you are loved by God no matter what. You are a child of the highest king. That settles it. Or at least it should in your mind.

In Exodus 23:25 the scripture states, "So you shall serve the Lord your God, and He will bless your bread and your water. I will take sickness away from the midst of you." God is giving us hints and clues from Genesis to Revelation of how to live the way that he designed for us. He is going to bless our food, so therefore we will not lack or live-in poverty or have a poverty mindset. He is going to take away sickness from us. I would say that is a great way to understand and follow his Word.

Sickness, disease (or dis-ease)

Satan is the creator of sickness and disease. The Word of God is the will of God and in John 10:10, Jesus said that "the thief [Satan] comes ONLY to kill, steal, and to destroy, but I have come [to give you life] and [for you] to have it more abundantly." (NKJV, emphasis mine) Psalm 34:19 says, "Many are the afflictions of the righteous, but the Lord delivers him out of them all. Afflictions are tests or trials, not sickness and disease. We are called to hold on to the confession of God's word. Not the sense of our feeling's. What God's word says should be the final authority. I do not have to deny that I feel a specific way, I just do not allow that feeling to rule and reign in my life and in my mind. We are all called to overflow with the Word of God. It should produce life, happiness, and health. It should overflow and pour out onto all those who we come into contact with. We should walk with spiritual fervor to resist whatever the devil attempts to place on us. Satan only can attempt to place things on us based on what he sees our reaction will be. And our confession should be, "I WILL PRAISE THE LORD NO MATTER WHAT."

When we praise the Lord on a continuous basis, we are throwing confusion into the enemy's camp. When we become determined to speak the Word of God only, great things will start to occur in our lives and around us.

2. Unhealthy relationships

Sometimes, through no fault of our own, we have associations with others that do not add value to our lives. Meaning, they are negative, unkind, demanding, or do not encourage us. Regardless of how they are associated or connected with us, we should be sure to distance ourselves from these kinds of relationships, or at least limit the time that we are with them. Instead of spending hours with someone who is negative, maybe only a quick conversation instead of an afternoon lunch. Let your goodness and positive remarks be the guiding factor of the conversation instead of their negativity.

We may not even realize it (most do not) that we are spiritually dying inside. We may have given up on our dreams because of lack of hope or faith. Whatever you had been believe for just is not happening as fast as you thought it should have, so you will just settle for the status quo. This is spiritual death of the potential that God has placed inside of you. If you speak that it will never happen, this is where your words become life or death to your spirit.

In several ways, God can use us to guide and help others if they find themselves in any one of the situations that I mentioned earlier. Sometimes the best conversations are the ones where we don't speak at all.

I have a beautiful daughter who was going through some things at school with some of the kids in her class. She was very upset about a matter, and she was telling me about the whole situation and talked and talked. Finally, she said," Mom why are you not saying anything?" I said, "Sometimes the best thing that I can say is to not say anything." She really needed to speak it out and process it to a kind, listening ear. We are not always supposed to be the ones doing all the talking. I believe that is why God gave us two ears and one mouth. We are all called to overflow with the Word of God. It is to produce life, happiness, and health. It is to overflow and pour out onto all those who I come into connect with. I am to walk with spiritual fervor to resist whatever the devil attempts to place on me. Satan only can attempt to place things on me based on what he sees my reaction is to be. I WILL PRAISE THE LORD NO MATTER WHAT.

This statement is worth repeating again, Satan is not creative in the areas he tries to trip us up. He will mainly attack you in three different areas. Your health, finances, and your relationship, either with your spouse, close family members or your children. It is the same old garbage that he tries to place on you. Along with these three, he will do his best to come against your confidence in the Word of God that you have in these areas. That is it. He is powerless. We need to remember that every time we open our mouths, we open the door to give him an edge by what we say. We can add to our demise by the simple words that we speak. We know that he is already defeated. Jesus did that for us on the cross. We are in a battle that has already been won. We are required to walk through it by faith, trusting and believing, knowing that the victory is already ours. We simply need to go through the process of acquiring the victory.

Proverbs 18:21(NKJV) says that "death and life are in the power of the tongue, and those who love it will eat its fruit." What is in your heart will come out of your mouth. If you have fear, unbelief or doubt in your heart, it will start to roll around in your head and then come out of your mouth. This can be a defining moment for you to physically place your hand over your mouth and say nothing. Keep silent unless you can speak words of faith, hope and belief. This is the instant moment—the exact time that you need to get into the Word of God. Read it. Hear it. Speak it out of your own mouth. Pray it. If your cup is running low or even on empty, you are in a very dangerous zone if you do not get your tank filled up and filled up fast. Depending on the battle or situation that you are dealing with, this may take some time. We speak too much and too often before we should. Use this as a time to keep quiet unless you are going to speak the Word.

We are to be imitators of God. (See Ephesians 5:1) We are to say what he tells us to say. If God would not say it over your situation, why are you saying it? Satan is spiritually blind. He is in darkness. I am not. I am a child of the light—of the King of all Kings. But Satan is watching all that I do, and he will attack me on the weak side. If I speak or act depressed or despondent, he will give me more of it. If I talk lack or failure, he will be very diligent to support that thought and give me more of that.

3. Spiritual Death

Let's talk a bit about Paul and his thorn in the flesh in 2 Corinthians 12:7-10. This has been so misunderstood for so many years and by so many people. First off, God is no respecter of people. If he promised us all his blessings in Deuteronomy 28 and stated in John 10:10 that he came to give us life, then why would sickness and disease be placed upon Paul? Search the Word. A messenger of Satan (v.7) means a personality, not a thing like sickness or disease. Sickness is not a messenger. Sickness is not a personality. A demon from hell was to buffet him. If you look up the word buffet, it means a blow with the hand, to pound repeatedly, to batter, to beat with repeated violent blows, to wear down or injure by hand use.

It was from Satan, not God. God does not employee demons from hell to promote his Word throughout the land. The purpose was to stop Paul from preaching the Word. It can be thought of as a "pain in the neck." Paul had to stand against this on a continuous basis. When Paul asked God three times to get this "thorn" off of him, God said, "My grace is sufficient for you." (v.9)

God was basically saying, "Paul, you got this thing. You have my favor. You have the authority over this messenger. I have given you the Holy Spirit, the comforter. Greater is he who is in you than this pesky pain in the neck. Rise above it, Paul. I am here to see you through it."

All of this was coming against Paul due to the Word, the revelation and knowledge that were given to him. He had a calling to get the Word out across nations. Satan wanted this stopped. It was because of the Word's sake. God was faithful to his Word. As you continue to look and research the Word, notice all of what Paul dealt with on a daily, regular basis. The Word said that he came out of them ALL. It never defeated him. This messenger of Satan did not stop the work of Paul and the Word of God from moving from area, region and around the world to be cherished even today for our growth and maturity in his Word.

Chapter 6

Gossip is Cancer

Gossip is a cancer. It is the cancer of the air. It is the most prevalent in our society. It is the elephant in the room that no one confronts but think is ok. We see it and hear it everywhere: social media, entertainment, even in our homes and churches. If it is not nice, do not say it—simply stated. The Word states that such as a man thinks, so he shall become. (See Proverbs 23:7) If you think something unkind, mean, negative, sarcastic, do not allow it to cross over the threshold of your lips. David spoke in Psalm 141:3 ESV says, "Set a guard, O Lord, over my mouth; keep watch over the door of my lips." There may be moments that you will have to physically place your hand over your mouth. That also means your thoughts, and your motives toward yourself and others. The heavens and earth were formed by the words that the Lord spoke. In Genesis 1:3 the Lord said let there be light, and it was so. So therefore, if we are to be imitators of Christ, which we are, in Ephesians 5:1 he not only instructs us to be just like him, he also calls us dear children. That is a term of endearment. How sweet is that! The creator of heaven, earth and all the galaxies and the universes calls us as close children to him. That goes to show us that he does want a personal and close relationship with each one of us. Not just a once-a-week relationship kind of thing.

The Bible also says we are justified by our words. "For by your words you will be justified, and by your words you will be condemned." (Matthew 12:37 ESV) This means an unfavorable or adverse judgment. Okay, I really don't want to put a sentence or a harsh treatment upon myself. I like the justified part—to provide something to be right or a good reason for actions. I want God to lean in and listen to my conversations and say, "Yes, that can and will be justified; look how she is lifting and building all situations around her and incorporating me into all that she is doing." That is what I want God to hear coming from my heart and mouth—statements of hope, praise, words of life. I want God to hear that I trust him, that I believe in his Word for me and my life. I will speak his Word and stand in faith and believe that he wrote that out for me and for my success.

Let's look at Proverbs 18:21 (NKJV): "Death and life are in the power of the tongue..." Notice that God has given us the authority over the course of our lives. Let's explore this...

God loves us so much that he has allowed us to make the decision as to whether we will honor, respect and be obedient to his Word. He gave us a choice. All throughout the ages, mankind has made the choice to either listen and follow his guide for our lives or go and do it on our own. We can observe this in Deuteronomy 28. It is a complete chapter on the blessings of obedience and the curses of disobedience. It is truly an eye opener when he breaks it down verse by verse. It is worth taking the time and read it over completely.

As we continue to study and meditate on his Word, we will also find again and again that even though we may go in a different direction, once we realize (as stated in Deuteronomy 28) that we have the power to choose the blessed life or the cursed life, he is always there to show us great mercy and grace. Then we will also realize that he truly wants what is best for us. However, there may be a consequence with our choices. We, as imitators of Christ, will be forgiven, however we will be called to walk it out. It is very interesting to study David in this aspect. He was known as a man after God's own heart (See Acts 13:22). Also, he was told that the sword would never leave his house, because of some of his choices (See 2 Samuel 12:10). This is such a wonderful example of how much God loves us—how much grace and mercy that he has bestowed upon us.

As we have completely explored the ins and outs of how our words will bring blessings or curses into our lives, we can then conclude that there are several examples of gossip that we can use as a guide to see the negative effects and evils of it.

In James 3, James refers to the tongue as the deadliest member of the body. We do have control over what we say. It starts in the thought pattern. Once you allow it to enter the "thought line up," it will generate fruit. That can be healthy, good, uplifting fruit or rotten, spoiled fruit. How does it get into the thought line up? Well, what are you reading? What types of things are you watching? Are they lifting your spirit? Is it based on what Paul told us to think about in Philippians 4:8 (whatever things are true, noble, just, pure…)? If not, why are you allowing it to consume your thoughts? What types of things are you listening to? Are you participating in the latest news at the office, at school… are you following social media and the negative blogs as if they were as powerful as the stock market? If so, STOP IT.

This is where seeds are being planted in your spirit. You are allowing the eye gate, the ear gate, and the mouth gate to swing wide open, and all kinds of bad influences are seeping into your spirit. This is where the gossip cancer is getting its fuel to start, and you just allow it to grow by each little thing that you pick up and see, hear or participate in.

You may say, well this is all around me. This is normal daily stuff that I encounter all the time—there is no way to avoid it. I cannot just turn off the news. I cannot just stop talking to the people that I go to work with or hang out with.

Well let me ask you this: If you had a loved one who was told that they had a terminal illness and the doctors told you that if you did x, y, z, that they would survive, would you go and do it to save their life? The answer is a resounding yes, of course you would!

So, you are no different. You are valuable in the eyes of God. You do deserve a life of favor and prosperity. You are a child of the highest King. You can be the change agent of that gossip cancer cell. You can be the one to change the conversation in the room. You can be the one to just get up and walk away from a negative conversation about someone.

How will you do this? Base all that you say and do on the Word of God. When you make that pinnacle decision that God is your source and that his Word will be the final authority in ALL areas of your life, this is the beginning of wisdom and your path to a successful, prosperous life. As I have stated, if you do not want it, do not say it.

Chapter 7

Who Has the Loudest Voice?

Did you know that the primary purpose of words is to release creative power into the situation, the state of current affairs, the atmosphere—not mere communication? Regardless of the language or dialect that you speak, God's instruction and Word to us are international. They are bound by no language barrier. The words and the arrangement of them, are a byproduct of the words that we speak. Most of society has no idea of the power of the spoken word. They simply believe that what they say is only for the here and now—that it has no effect on the future. Many say things off the cuff or simply say what they feel without giving any thought to what they speak at all.

Here is a simple list of common sayings that you may think are no big deal, but the results can be deadly. Remember in Proverbs 18:21, "Death and life are in the power of the tongue...." The words are in your mouth. Not God's. Not Satan's. It is what *you* say.

Common sayings of our culture:

It is what it is.

Counter scripture: Romans 4:17, "calling those things which are not as they are."

That just tickles me pink.

Counter scripture: Nehemiah 8:10, "...The joy of the Lord is [my] strength."

We have more month than money.

Counter scripture: Philippians 4:19, "...God shall supply all [my] need according to his riches in glory by Christ Jesus."

I am a realist. I am just calling things as I see them.

Counter scripture: Romans 4:17, "Calling those things which are not as though they are."

I am just thrilled to death.

Counter scripture: Romans 15:13, "Now may the God of hope fill you with all joy and peace as you trust in him, so that you may overflow with hope by the power of the Holy Spirit."

It's the same old thing. Today is the same, day in and day out.

Counter scriptures: Isaiah 43:19, "Behold, I am doing a new thing; now it springs forth, do you not perceive it? I will make a way in the wilderness and rivers in the desert."

2 Corinthians 5:17, "Therefore, if anyone is in Christ, he is a new creation. The old has gone, the new has come."

This is as good as it's going to get.

Counter scripture: 1 Corinthians 2:9, "...Eye has not seen, nor ear has heard what God has in store for his children that he loves."

How are you today? Pretty good, under the circumstances. (Who wants to be under the weight of the world?)

Counter scripture: Psalm 18:33," You make my feet run as fast as those of a deer, and you help me stand on the mountains."

Another day, another dollar.

Counter scriptures: Philippians 4:19, "...God shall supply all [my] need according to his riches in glory by Christ Jesus."

Proverbs 13:22, "A good person leaves an inheritance for their children's children."

This is just a rat race I am living in, day in and day out. Nothing seems to change and get better.

Counter scripture: Hebrews12:1, "Therefore we also, since we are surrounded by so great a cloud of witnesses, let us lay aside every weight, and the sin which so easily ensnares us, and let us run with endurance the race that is set before us."

I just love this, or I just love that.

Counter scripture: 1 John 2:15, "Do not love the world or anything in the world. If anyone loves the world, love for the Father is not in them."

I am just dying to _____ (fill in the phrase).

Counter scripture: Proverbs 18:21, "the power of death and life are in the tongue."

It would be a joy to go.

Counter scripture: Nehemiah 8:10, "The joy of the Lord is my strength."

My body is killing me. My back is killing me. My joints are killing me. My job is killing me. My kids will be the death of me. I have a headache, and it is killing me. (Stop aiding and abetting death by your words or popular sayings at the time.)

Counter scriptures: John 10:10, "The thief does not come EXCEPT to steal, and to kill, and to destroy. I have come that they may have life, and that they may have it more abundantly."

Proverbs 18:21, "Death and life are in the power of [MY] tongue, and he who delights in it eats the fruit thereof."

I am just telling you what's going on with them so that we can properly pray for them.

Counter scripture: Proverbs 18:8, "The words of a gossip are like choice morsels; they go down to the inmost parts."

You win a few, you lose a few.

Counter scripture: Psalm 27:6, "Now my head will be lifted up above my enemies, even those who surround me. I will sacrifice in his tent with shouts of joy; I will sing and make melodies to the Lord."

Another day another dollar for me to complain and holler.

Counter scripture: Psalm 45:1, "My heart is moved by a noble theme as I recite my verses to the king. My tongue is the pen of a skillful writer."

When we engage and speak these common phrases on a regular basis and then pray and ask God for help and guidance and nothing changes, we blame God. It is not

God's fault that we are living under our potential that he has in store for us. This is our doing.

What we pray and what we speak on a continuous regular basis should lineup with each other. We are to focus on the promise of the greater glory. Not the problem. Not the adversity.

I will learn how to speak God's Word as affirmations over my situation. Here are a few ways and examples of the proper way to speak over your life and your situations:

Praise God for his goodness and his power and his glory.

There is purity of my mouth in your Word. There is financial peace and security in your Word. I speak to the mountain, then the mountain will begin to move. I praise the Lord first then the mountain will move.

Psalm 145 is a wonderful Psalm to speak over your day. Also, John 16:33 is a good reminder: "trust me, you will be unshakable and assured, deeply at peace. In this godless world you will continue to experience difficulties. But take heart! I have conquered the world."

He also shared a promise with us in Deuteronomy 8:18 (NKJV); "And you shall remember the Lord your God, for it is he who gives you the ability to produce wealth, that he may establish his covenant which he swore to your fathers, as it is this day."

He loves us so much that in Proverbs 10:22 he reassures us that his blessings make life rich; nothing we do can improve on God.

He wants us to really get a hold of what he has in store for our lives. He even started with the promise to us in Genesis 12:2 (MSG): "I'll make you a great nation and bless you. I'll make you famous; you'll be a blessing; I'll bless those who bless you; those who curse you I'll curse all the families of the earth will be blessed through you." Wow, that is an amazing promise if we decide to grab hold of that by faith.

In conclusion, which voice is the loudest in your head? The voice that tells you to speak what the rest of society is speaking? Or listening to the voice of faith and your future?

Chapter 8

Stand Firm on the Word

There have been so many different teachings on goals. Good goals. Great goals. Awesome goals. Big Hairy Audacious Goals. What really is a goal? Does God even care, or is he concerned with your goals? Is it OK to have several different kinds of goals? The answer is yes, yes and a BIG yes. Amen!

You also may ask, *what does having a goal have to do with standing firm on the Word mean?* It means never giving up on your goal if it takes longer than you think it should take. *But how is this related to my foundation that I have with my relationship with God?* Glad you asked...

God made us and created us to dream and to really dream big. Look at all that he created in just six days; and we are, by faith, adopted into his kingdom. We are to think the way he thinks. The brain is a goal-seeking organ. When you set a goal, you are giving your brain a picture—a connection point of what is churning in your spirit to become a reality. It is the wonderful gift of where you are now and propelling yourself to where you would like to go. You see, your brain thinks in pictures.

It does not know the difference between the pictures that you place in your mind. It will automatically gravitate to the image that you have created. What you continue to think about you will bring about.

If you are able to achieve your goals within your own efforts and strengths, your goals are too small. If this is the case, why do you need God? I want this book to challenge you to step out of the boat and walk in faith—trust God for the big dreams that you have in your heart. If you have buried them deep inside of you because of age, too much time has gone by, or… [any other excuse that you can insert here], it is time to dust them off, get them out of the closet and start to dream big again.

I regularly hang my goals inside the bathroom closet. I see them every morning as I am getting ready. I also write my goals on my bathroom mirror with a dry erase marker. I see them daily and I speak them out daily. Well, over time, the goal that I had hung in my closet started to collect dust, in more ways than one. (I do not dust my closet that much.) I also was not speaking over it on a daily basis; therefore, I started to believe that it would never happen. Many years have passed since I first wrote that goal down. I did not continue to speak over it or water it with words of faith and encouragement. So, it also started to get dusty in my spirit. The thought started to come up. *It will never happen. It is a pipe dream. I am not good enough to make that goal happen. I have been trying to make it happen too long. So, what is the use?* Does any of this sound familiar?

Recently, as I was dusting out my closet, I saw the goal written out on paper on the side of the wall. The Holy Spirit quietly spoke to me and said, "It is time to get your dream out of the closet." You see I have a part to play in this coming to pass. I still see the goal as impossible in my own strength. However, I have a new sense of excitement that it will come to pass. Why? God told me to believe that he will fulfill the desires of my heart. He says that in Mathew 6:33: "But seek first the kingdom of God and his righteousness, and all these things will be added to you." (ESV)

Here is where most of us get stuck. (I am speaking from personal experience.) I will read this scripture and think, *sure that sounds great, but will he do it for me? I am sure all things are possible to those who believe. But how will he do it?* It is none of our concern how God will do it. We simply need to believe that he can, and he will because he said so and he loves us.

I had to change my thinking about this specific goal and start to speak as if it was already done. My part of the goal changed what I was telling myself. If you constantly tell yourself that you will always be on the heavy side physically, you will. If you believe that you will never achieve that raise or drive that kind of a car, you are programming your brain in what direction to go. You need to practice setting goals on a daily, regular basis. From small ones to what has been referred to as "big, out-of-this-world, only done by the hand of God goals... A goal needs to make you quiver at the thought of it coming to pass. If the goal is achievable by your own efforts, then why do you need vision like God's? Why would you need God at all? Because when you set a goal that you can achieve on your own, you are not living up to all that God created you to be. When you set a goal that you even back away from, then that is what you need to go after. By investing your imagination in this manner, you are allowing and equipping your faith to become activated.

Walt Disney was known to approach his board of directors with all kinds of ideas and vision. When he presented an idea and they agreed with him and said, "Yes, Walt we can do that," he would respond with "No let's not do it." When he presented an idea that they said to him was impossible, he said, "That is exactly what we will do."

You need vision like God's because he wants us to think like he said in Ephesians 3:20 (my paraphrase): "God can do anything far more than you could ever imagine or guess or request in your wildest dreams." Wow! That is in God's Word. That is God telling us that if we can imagine it on our own, it is not big enough. God is telling us, "Dream bigger, think bigger, imagine your wildest dreams, and that is where I can start to work for you in your life." I don't know about you, but as I re-read that, I get excited because I feel like God is saying to me, "Sherry, you are dreaming too small. Trust me, try me, prove me if I will not pour out my blessing from heaven over top of you and your family." And my response is, "Lord, I am ready; let the blessings start to down pour."

If we really will be honest with ourselves, every goal or dream needs to first be birthed and covered in prayer. God is the one who made you and created you. He is the one that placed some of those desires inside of you.

As I have been studying and researching for this book, I thought that everyone had the same goals that I had. I really have had to deal with the thoughts, *what is the use? Someone else has the same goal—let that person rise to the occasion and they can do it. Honestly, I am getting tired; I have waited for so long. How much longer must I wait to see this come to pass? I guess my life is good enough where it is now. Someone else can do it.* NO. NO. NO A THOUSAND TIMES OVER—NO!

All that negative self-doubt and self-talk are coming from the pit of hell to get you off track from your destiny of making a huge difference in other people's lives. You are called to be a distribution center—to give to others. God has given you that goal, and he expects you to finish it and complete it for the glory of his kingdom.

Think of it like this: goal setting is the ability to give your brain homework to work on every day until you see the final result. Meaning you get an A when it shows up. How cool is that? Since your brain thinks in pictures, start to tell it what to focus on along with what you are saying about those dreams and visions. If you desire to own your own company and give 50% of the earnings to missions, then that is what you will drive your brain to think on. You will think of a way to market your service or product. You will ask God to send the right people to work with you. You will ask God to send the right people to be your customers and on and on.

Think of it like this: When you sow a thought, you will receive a harvest in action. You think that no one will come to your event. That is what you will get. You think that you will never lose that last 10 pounds. Then you will never lose that weight. You think that you are not pretty enough or good enough and no one will want to marry you, then you will receive what you are expecting. You think that you will never be debt free and own your own cars, own your homes, you never will. Whatever you think, your life will go in that direction. It may take time; it may happen quickly. Whichever path, it will come to pass just as you think that it would. But when you step out in faith and believe what God says about you, how he wants to bless you and how he has a prosperous plan for you, then that will become the primary thoughts in your mind. It all begins on the inside of you.

Declare out of your mouth what you would like to have, not what you see.

It is a biblical concept. God is the one who came up with the idea of calling those things which are not into existence, into the light. Use the Word of God as affirmations to speak over your life daily.

In the final chapters I will provide you with a list of affirmations to speak out on a daily basis; but here are a couple of examples to get started on so you can practice making this a habit. (Yes, it must become a habit!)

I declare God's incredible blessings over my life. I will see an explosion of God's goodness and a sudden widespread increase.

I will experience the surpassing greatness of God's favor. It will elevate me to a level higher than I ever dreamed of. Explosive blessings are coming my way.

We as children of God are to focus on the promise of the greater glory. Not the problem. Not the adversity.

Having faith in the foundation of God's Word is the true success that you need for your life—in all areas of your life. We are called to have an unwavering faith in what God has promised to us. We are to lean into, press on and stand firm to trust his Word in the face of all contradictory and opposing circumstances. There will be weapons formed against us. OK, take a moment and think what is he talking about: weapons formed against us? What are "weapons" that can used against us in our lives today?

Remember, Satan is not creative. He only uses three basic areas to try to unravel us or get us off our game, per se. These areas bear repeating:

1. Health: Yours, family or close friend
2. Finances: Personal day-to-day, able to provide for others, business/investments
3. Relationships: Family, friends, co-workers or in the church setting

Think about it: In all three areas it could be family, friends, coworkers, classmates, roommates, or members of the body of Christ to get you off believing, standing, and trusting God's word.

The Word guarantees us that they will not overtake us. The weapons—these modern-day issues—can be formed, sharpened, and even taken up against us. They will not prevail over us. It is a promise and guarantee that God has given to us. You will find this reference in Isaiah 54:17: "No weapon formed against you shall prosper, and every tongue which rises against you in judgement you shall condemn. This is the heritage of the servants of the Lord and their righteousness is from me."

Take this concept into complete context as to what this whole book is about. Do not let your mouth be used as a weapon against. Guard it as if your life depends upon it. According to the Word, it does.

Having faith in God and his Word is the true secret of success. Faith that dares you to press your toes to the line divides those who walk by faith and those who talk about faith. It is better to be a wet water walker, than a dry boat talker.

God is waiting for you to take that first step of faith. He is there to place his super on your *natural* ability. He will cause us to be victorious over any trail, any circumstance and any difficulty that may come along.

When you have made the commitment to walk by faith, you have made the decision to never, never, quit or give up. If you are backed up in a corner and you can only see one step in front of you, then faith will assist you with that one step. Then you will have the Word of God to be able to make that next step. God will be there for each one. God is a God of creating a "suddenly" in our lives. Taking that one step of faith can be all that it takes for your miracle to appear and turn it all around in that moment. It can produce the joy of the Lord and fulfill the promise of God in your life. By simply being obedient and doing the Word, you will strengthen your faith. Remember, faith comes by hearing the Word of God. (See Romans 10:17) And He's given us all the measure of faith. (See Romans 12:3 KJV)

And without faith, it is impossible to please God, as it says in Hebrews 11:6. But we do have a part to make that faith grow.

You will arrive as a success. God does not create failure. God is a creator of joy and good things. Success in all areas of your life means a strong commitment to God and his Word. When you position yourself and purpose in your heart to please God, he will give you the desires of your heart. (See Psalm 37:4)

Many times in life we are presented with something like the wall that Nehemiah had to rebuild (See Nehemiah 2). It looked impossible. He had to stand strong even before he knew what he was called to do. He had to walk by faith when no one was walking with him.

He had a full-time job in Persia, in the king's court. He was the cup bearer to King Artaxerxes. This was a high-ranking position in the palace at that time. He tasted and drank everything before it was presented to the king. Poisoning and removing the current ruler in authority at that time was very common.

Nehemiah had to ask for time off from his job. He was in a different area of the province at this time. He was not close to his hometown that had experienced the damage and ruin.

He was told that the walls of the city were completely destroyed and that the city itself and all the inhabitants were exposed to robbers and vandalism. It was gravely unprotected.

But Nehemiah did not even know currently how bad the damage was. He was going off a report that his friends told him. It states in Nehemiah chapter 1 that it was over half a century since the temple was restored—that the walls were still in disarray. That is 50 years. That means he had not been back to his homeland in that length of time. Let's pause here for a moment and think of this as it plays out. Would you commit to restore something that you have not seen in over 50 years?

He spent time in prayer first, asking God what he was to do with the new information that he just received. Once he spent time fasting and praying, then he went to the king.

How many times do we just *do* before we stop, ask, seek God's direction, and wait to listen for the answer? More times than we all would like to admit. I know I can say that for myself.

Nehemiah went to the king, who was pagan and did not believe in the God that Nehemiah believed in. He told the king that he was distraught and needed to do this; and he gave the king a deadline of when it would be completed.

The king granted him his request with favor as he passed through the lands to get to his destination.

During this time Nehemiah dealt with depression. He felt overwhelmed, and enemies and his workers were trying to kill him. Hit men were sent to take Nehemiah out. But Nehemiah drew his strength from knowing that he was in the center of God's will, which helped him overcome. Talk about standing strong against all odds! Attempts were made to cut off his supplies, and the people who were on the wall with him started to turn against him. They wanted to quit, and then on top of

ALL of this, they had to build with one hand and fight off enemies with a weapon in the other hand.

Yet, the Word says that they had a heart and mind to work. That is amazing! They wanted to kill their leader. However, they were willing to work and fight at the same time to restore what was taken from them by the enemy over 50 years ago. Not sure if this hits you like it hit me.

We have not because we ask not (See James 4:2b), then when we do ask, we grumble and complain about what God is giving us because it is just not good enough and we may have to "work for it" or "get a little dirty" or "get a little uncomfortable."

I am humbled by the revelation that I found. This is one of those Sunday school lessons that we hear growing up; however, it brought a whole new meaning to me as I was studying it out.

1. Nehemiah saw a need. He asked God what should be done and stepped up to the plate to do something about it.
2. Nehemiah set a goal of when it would be done.
3. Nehemiah looked over what needed to be done in the darkness of the night.
4. Nehemiah had a team that partnered with him on the cause at hand.

5. 52 days later the impossible was completed!

Because one man said to God, "Pick me, I will go. I will circle this impossible situation, and I will apply my natural abilities so that your supernatural abilities will shine through and you will get all the glory for this."

My prayer: “Oh God, give me the spirit of Nehemiah that I will see as you see, and I will step up to the plate and will do as you would have me to do.”

Chapter 9

Control Your Tongue

This is so much easier said than done. Have you ever been around positive people? In a great atmosphere, you are ignited with joy and happiness, and you think, *I've got this. I know that I will be able to handle any situation if it ever comes up.* Can you hear me laughing out loud? Because I have said this very thing! "Oh, I am a solid warrior of faith, I am a woman of God, I can control my tongue in any situation." Matthew 13 is the parable about the sower who sows the seed. As you may know, the seed that the birds steal symbolizes Satan, who comes immediately to steal the Word that you just received.

He does not want you to have the revelation and knowledge that we cannot control our tongue on our own. Maybe you are like me, who thought for years that I could handle it on my own. I thought, "Really, it is just simple plain words. It is no big deal. Nobody remembers what I say anyway." Sorry to disappoint you, but I had been learning the hard way.

There is power in each word that you speak. God said in the Word that you will have to give an account of every idle word that is spoken (See Matthew 12:36).

Not sure how you feel about that, but when I think that through, I feel sick thinking of all the things that I have said that I did not think mattered. I went to the Word to figure out how to clean my mouth up spiritually and in the natural realm. Satan has assigned little imps to follow you around to catch every word that you say. When we say things like "That makes me *sick to death.*" "That *scared me to death*" we think it is no big deal. But over time they add up and there is a record made against us. To clear your past and your slate: say this with me out loud," IN THE NAME OF JESUS, I BIND YOU SATAN AND YOUR EVIL TATICS AGAINIST ME. YOU HAVE NO AUTHORITY OR POWER OVER ME OR MY FUTURE. BY THE BLOOD OF JESUS AND THE AUTHORITY THAT HE GAVE TO ME WHEN HE WENT TO THE CROSS, I WIPE IT ALL CLEAR AND MY PAST WILL NOT HAUNT OR HURT ME EVER AGAIN. GLORY TO GOD. THANK YOU, JESUS."

This may never have happened to you, however, I will be transparent with you and share how I have had to walk through this one. There was a time when I was not being nice to my kids, and I am telling you that the spit was flying and the veins were bulging out of my neck and at that given moment, the phone rang. Of course, I answered it oh so sweetly, "Hello, this is Sherry." Once I realized what I was doing. I thought, "Lord, you have your work cut out with me. When will I ever get this right?" I felt like such a bad mom at that given moment.

We have to depend on God daily to help us control not only the words that we speak but also the tone and of what we are saying.

Stop speaking what you want and start speaking like you already have it; call those things which are not as though they are. (See Romans 4:17) Speak the Word only. That is the Word of the Lord only.

Psalm 62:5-6 in The Message translation says it best: "God, the one and only—I'll wait as long as he says. Everything I hope for comes from him, so why not?" "He's solid rock under my feet, breathing room for my soul, an impregnable castle: I'm set for life."

Decide to not be moved until it comes to pass. It does not matter what you may think about a situation. You hold onto what the Word says about it.

Make this declaration: "I believe this is a vision from God. I believe this is a dream from God. I know that I know that he is guiding me and leading me in the direction that I shall go."

Between receiving the Word and seeing it fulfilled in that gap of time, you must determine in your heart, mind, and spirit that quitting is not an option. You need to have this mindset. We as a society have such a "fast food" mindset. We pray it. We want to see it show up, well you know, like now!

In Genesis, God said that he has given us seed, time and harvest. (See Genesis 8:22) I believe that we need to break that apart. We have a dream, idea, vision—something that we believe has been placed down in our spirits to achieve from God; like this book, which has been 18 years in the making. Some of my thoughts over the years have been, *why would I want to write a book? English was not my strongest subject in school. Who would want to read anything that I have to say? I am not a pastor, evangelist or even a minister of a church. I have not been to Bible college or received any formal training at all. I am really a nobody who no one has heard of.* Even with all these negative thoughts that were standing in my way and constantly in my mind, I had to bring all of them captive to the obedience of Christ. (See 2 Corinthians 10:5) Meaning, I could not shake the idea that God wanted me to write this book. I finally decided: I am going to finish this book. I will be obedient to God. I will push aside all my fears, hesitations and just do it. I will do it for God and God alone. As I said earlier, I do not want to get to heaven and God says to me, "I asked you to write books for me; why did you not do it?" "Well, you know God. I am busy. I am a mom, wife, business owner, motivational speaker. I just did not have time to create it or make it happen." As you could imagine, I do not want to live with that weighing heavily on me.

I even laugh at the idea that once this gets into print that I can shove this in the face of Satan and say, "Just watch me now. You will not stop, hold up or prevent the Word of God inside of me. It is to pour out and help others who need to hear that I walked through this. I am an overcomer in Christ Jesus. Satan, by me publishing this book, if someone else will rise up, and step over the line from fear to faith and achieve what has been placed in their heart, then so be it!"

When I speak the Word of God only, it creates an expectation within me. I say to myself, "I will not be moved." I get extremely excited thinking that it is OK for me to expect things from God. I think, *Am I good enough? Good enough to prosper at my marriage? Good enough to be the mom that I have been called to be? Good enough to oversee a multimillion-dollar consultant team? Good enough to do all that I feel I need to do in the Kingdom of God?*

Yes, is the answer to all these questions, and so it is with you.

Something else that I have discovered along the way is that first I had to understand that the journey and the process of getting to my vision, goal or dream was to enjoy the "path" that I was on at that given moment. I am a get-it-done type of person, and I really had to look around and enjoy the moment and the season or I would have missed so many steps to getting where I wanted to land. Second, because I decided that Jesus Christ was my Lord and Savior, I was most assuredly, "good enough." Once I realize that it was OK to ask him all questions concerning all things from the biggest obstacles to the smallest details, I started to really relax, let go and enjoy who I was becoming in the process.

I realized that I was becoming better and stronger each day. I also realized that by taking one step, one moment, one day at a time, I would arrive at my destiny. But the benefit would be that I would arrive much happier, and many more people would be with me along the journey as well, instead of me spearheading it to the top all alone.

I have studied Mark 11:22-24 many times over the years, and the funny thing is that when I thought that I had gotten it (understood it), I realized that I had only scratched the surface of it.

Jesus said in verse 22, "Have faith in God." That is pretty simple and straightforward. Not anything too complicated about that. You would think, have faith in God. It does not say, "Have faith in yourself"; it is in God. Similarly, it doesn't say, "Have faith in your job"; "Have faith in your spouse"; "Have faith in your employer"; "Have faith in the economy"; "Have faith in the government:"

We are to **have faith in God**—and in him alone.

Let me ask you, how many times have we put our faith in all these other areas, and when they fail us, then we will decide to have faith in God? Why do we leave God as a last-ditch effort? I know that I have. I have told myself so many times, "I will work harder. I will do more in myself, and my company will notice it. I will do more around the house so that my family will notice it. Then they will love me more." Trust me; it does not work that way. Simply have faith in God. I am still working on this one. When I go to God first and ask him how to work something out, then everything thing else will fall into place quite nicely.

In Mark 11:23, Jesus said to speak to the mountain. *What? Now he wants me to talk to a big heaping mound of dirt! What good will that do? What does that really mean?* What in your life appears to be so huge and out of control that it truly takes your breath away? You feel like you cannot handle one more thing. This would be a mountain in your life. Finances, health, relationships at work or at home? There are mountains that he wants us to speak to. When I speak to my mountain to be removed, I believe that my words will come to pass. There is a force behind my words. I am sending them into the atmosphere as a force to penetrate the darkness—a force to split apart the fear, doubt, unbelief, and the self-destructive words. My words are a force to split the darkness from the light. The reality is that I am either held in bondage or set free by my words. I can rise to be one of the greats who will use my faith to move Satan's tactics out of my way.

What comes out of our mouths determine our success or failure. I know that this sounds simple; however, the Word of God and his instructions to us as his children generally are very straightforward.

I would like to finish this chapter with the amazing scripture that I found in The Message translation of Amos 9:13: "Yes indeed, it won't be long now." God's Decree. "Things are going to happen so fast your head will swim, one thing fast on the heels of the other. You won't be able to keep up. Everything will be happening at once—and everywhere you look, blessings!"

Oh, glory to God. Isn't that just beautiful?

You plant your seed—the words that you speak. You allow God's Word and time to water that goal, dream, vision, or instruction from God. Before you know it, it will show up right on time. You are standing on the Word, placing a guard over your mouth. You are willing to wait for as long as it takes; it will not take too long. You must determine that giving up is not an option.

Chapter 10

Words of Wisdom

Death and life are in the power of the tongue, and those who love it will eat its fruit. (Proverbs 18:21 NKJV)

Words kill, or words give life; they are either poison or fruit—you choose. You know the statement that says, "Sticks and stones may break my bones, but words will never hurt me"? This is ONE of the biggest lies that our society has believed, and it comes out of the pit of hell! Words have done more damage to marriages, homes, dreams, visions, churches, self-esteem, and anything else that you can think of to stop people from believing and truly living the life that God has intended for them.

When you feel that your life is starting to veer off course from where you believe that God has directed you, I encourage you to write down these verses and read them out loud to yourself over your situation. Take these words of God as you would take medicine; morning and evening… as often as the Lord tells you. (See Proverbs 4:20-22)

Satan will come and use all types of distractions to lead you off course. Most of the time it is very subtle, and you will not even realize it at the time. You will need to cover a lot of ground to get you back where God wants you to be. Satan is a very patient enemy. He is watching your every move, and he will steal from you a little here and a little there if you do not keep your guard up.

Praise God that we have simple instruction (a.k.a. God's Word) for everyday life to use as a guide to keep us on track. Here are some key verses to as weapons against Satan's tactics:

Proverbs 10:11 The mouth of a good person is a deep, life-giving well, but the mouth of the wicked is a dark cave of abuse.
Be aware of what you are attracting with your words.

Proverbs 10:12 Hatred starts fights, but love pulls a quilt over the bickering.
Love covers all.

Proverbs 10:18 Liars secretly hoard hatred: fools openly spread slander.
If a gossip and liar lie to you about someone else, they will gossip and lie about you.

Proverbs 11:13A gossip betrays a confidence, but a trustworthy person keeps a secret.
A true friend is a forever friend.

Proverbs 12:13 The gossip of bad people gets them in trouble, the conversation of good people keeps them out of it.
Be aware of who you hang out with.

Proverbs 13: 2 The good acquire a taste for helpful conversation: bullies push and shove their way through life.
Be kind to each other.

Proverbs 15:2 Knowledge flows like spring water from the wise, fools are leaky faucets, dripping nonsense.
Many words can be a waste of your breath.

Proverbs 18:20 Words satisfy the mind as much as fruit does the stomach; good talk is as gratifying as a good harvest.
Good uplifting words are the only ones that you should be using.

Proverbs 16:27-28 Mean people spread mean gossip; their words smart and burn.

Troublemakers start fights; gossips break up friendships. Guard what you say, even if you think no one is listening.

Proverbs 17:9 Love prospers when a fault is forgiven, dwelling on it separates close friends.
Even the smallest hurts and offenses can be damaging.

Proverbs 26:20 When you run out of wood, the fire goes out: when the gossip ends, the quarrel dies down.
Simply stop talking if it is not encouraging or uplifting.

Proverbs 29:11 A fool lets it all hang out; a sage quietly mulls it over.
Silence is golden.

Proverbs 13:3 Whoever guards his mouth preserves his life; he who opens wide his lips comes to ruin.
Simply said, some things are left better unsaid.

Proverbs 15:1 A soft answer turns away wrath, but a harsh word stirs up anger.
When you can control your words, you can control the atmosphere of your surroundings.

Proverbs 15:4 Kind words heal and help; cutting words wound and harm.
Be careful little mouth what you speak.

Proverbs 21:23 Watch your words and hold your tongue; you will save yourself a lot of grief.
Wars can be avoided when we keep quiet.

Proverbs 29:20 Do you see a man who is hasty in his words? There is more hope for a fool than for him.
Pride goes before a fall.

Proverbs 17: 27-28 The one who knows much says little; an understanding person remains calm. Even dunces who keep quiet are thought to be wise; as long as they keep their mouths shut, they are smart.
Appearances can be deceiving.

Proverbs 25:11 A word fitly spoken is like apples of gold in a setting of silver.
The right word at the right time is like a custom-made piece of jewelry, and a wise friend's timely reprimand is like a gold ring slipped on your finger.

Proverbs 11:12 Whoever belittles his neighbor lacks sense, but a man of understanding remains silent.
You have to live next to your neighbor.

Proverbs 27:2 Don't call attention to yourself; let others do that for you.

No one likes a bragger.

Proverbs 18:13 Answering before listening is both stupid and rude.
God gave us all two ears and one mouth for a reason.

Proverbs 10:19 The more talk, the less truth, the wise measure their words.
Less is better.

Ephesians 4:29 Watch the way you talk. Let nothing foul or dirty come out of your mouth. Say only what helps, each word is a gift.
Words can influence the heart of the matter.

Ephesians 5:4 Though some tongues just love the taste of gossip, those who follow Jesus have better uses for language than that. Don't talk dirty or silly. That kind of talk does not fit our style. Thanksgiving is our dialect.
Make all your words count.

Colossians 3:8-9 But now you must put them all away; anger, wrath, malice, slander, and obscene talk (profanity & dirty talk) from your mouth.
Always speak kindly to others.

Colossians 4:6 Be gracious in your speech. The goal is to bring out the best in others in a conversation, not put them down, not cut them out.
Do your best to find something to say that is good about that person.

James 3:1-2 Don't be in any rush to become a teacher, my friends. Teaching is highly responsible work. Teachers are held to the strictest standards. And none of us are perfectly qualified. We get it wrong nearly every time we open our mouths. If you could find someone whose speech was perfectly true, you'd have a perfect person, in perfect control of life.
No one has arrived at this level yet if they say that they "know it all"; give their instruction little weight.

James 3: 3-5 A bit in the mouth of a horse controls the whole horse. A small rudder on a huge ship in the hands of a skilled captain sets a course in the face of the strongest winds.
A word out of your mouth may seem of no account, but it can accomplish nearly anything—or destroy it!

James 3:5-6 It only takes a spark, remember, to set off a forest fire. A careless of wrongly placed word out of your mouth can do that. By our speech we can ruin the world, turn harmony to chaos, throw mud on a

reputation, send the whole world up in and go up in smoke with it, smoke right from the pit of hell.
We create our worlds with our words.

James 3: 7-10 This is scary: you can tame a tiger, but you cannot tame a tongue- it's never been done. The tongue runs wild, a wanton killer. With our tongues we bless God our Father, with the same tongue we curse the very men and women he made in his image. Curses and blessings out of the same mouth.
You have the power in your mouth to change your life and those around you.

James 3: 10-12 My friends, this can't go on. A spring doesn't gush fresh water one day and brackish the next, does it? Apple trees don't bear strawberries, do they? Raspberry bushes don't bear apples, do they? You're not going to dip into a polluted mud hole and get a cup of clear, cool water, are you?
You will get what you speak, every time.

James 1:19 Let every person be quick to hear, slow to speak, slow to anger.
We are to listen twice as much as we speak.

James 1:26 If anyone thinks he is religious and does not bridle his tongue but deceives his heart, this person's religion is worthless.
God did not create religion, man instituted that.

Proverbs 16:24 Gracious words are like a honeycomb, sweetness to the soul and health to the body.
You attract what you speak.

Chapter 11

Affirmations to Speak

When God wanted something to happen or occur in his creation, he spoke it. We see that all the way back in Genesis where he created the universes. We, by faith are his chosen children and should expect the same results when we speak something into existence.

God also instructs us in his Word to meditate on the Word both day and night. To meditate means to consider or to think over carefully; contemplate to spend time in quiet thinking; reflect.

According to 2 Corinthians 10:5, we are instructed to renew our minds daily and to bring every thought into captivity according to the obedience of Christ. Daily. It is that simple. Daily. We are to consider God's Word over our situations. Daily. We are to be speaking his promises over ourselves. Again, out of the abundance of the heart the mouth speaks. (See Luke 6:45)

You have come this far on this journey with me—will you take it one step further?

Will you take the time on a daily basis to speak into existence what you are believing to happen vs. what you "see" with your natural eyes? Are you willing to step out in faith and "see" with your spiritual eyes that God has provided for you in his book of promises?

In the final chapters of this book, I have provided you with affirmations you can speak over your life daily. Ponder on one or more of them daily. Really let them sink deep down into your heart and spirit. Also speak them out loud. You believe yourself more than you believe the words that anyone speaks to you. You are the master of your being; you are in charge of the thoughts that you entertain and the words that you speak. What you allow your mind to rest upon daily is completely up to you.

Let's get started on the path to changing your future, one word at a time, and one day at a time.

1. I'm created in God's image. I resemble my Father because He created me in His own image. I am beautiful. (Genesis 1:27)
2. I welcome today with great anticipation and joy of the good things you have prepared for me.
3. I like who I am and who I am becoming.
4. I am known by God. He has engraved me on the palms of His hands. (Isaiah 49:16)

5. Right now, today, I am capable of giving myself the gift of complete self-assurance, self-belief, and nonstop confidence in who I am.
6. I greet today with great excitement of the good and prosperous things you have prepared for me.
7. I have been redeemed and my mouth will proclaim it. God has redeemed me from the hand of the enemy, and I am saying so. (Psalm 107:2)
8. Teach me your ways today so that I may walk in the authority that you have equipped me with to honor and glorify you.
9. Grant me the ability to clearly hear your words and instruction as you give me insight, ideas, and ways to prosper my surroundings.
10. Cease the arrows shot toward me by day and the thoughts of terror by night to completely come to an end. I have peace in my spirit, day, and night.
11. Today is a good day to put all doubts, fears, and unbelief about myself behind me. Today is a new day for me to create a new me.
12. Thank you for making me fearfully and wonderfully made in your likeness. God, you love me.
13. I have a good reputation. There is nothing negative about me. You have given me a new day and a fresh new start.

14. I am blessed. God has put his hand of blessings upon me. He has commanded me to be prosperous in all areas of my life today. (Genesis 1:28)
15. Today is a great day. I have what it takes. I choose to do it right, to do it well. I choose to live today with joy and love.
16. I have no need to make excuses. I gladly take responsibility to change my mindset and my future.
17. I speak peace and joy into my life, relationships, workplace, and every situation that I encounter.
18. I have joy. I accept that I am not a victim of the circumstances of my life. I create the winning life that I live. I am the penman of my day. I create my day by the words that I speak.
19. I take full responsibility for everything about me. I take control of every thought that I have. I think good about myself and my situations on purpose.
20. I know that I am headed in the right direction today. I have drive, determination, endurance, and stamina. I have a winning attitude about myself and about everything that I do.
21. I am stronger today than what I was yesterday; physically, financially, emotionally, and spiritually. Today is a new day.

22. I choose to live my life by choice, not by chance. I am working on becoming a better me every day.
23. Anything or anyone who crosses my path today, that tries to hurt, stop, frustrate, hinder, or come against me, I command to be moved out of my path in the name of Jesus.
24. I am practical and realistic. I believe in the best possible outcome of any situation that I will face today. I have what it takes to make today a great day.
25. I respect myself. I respect my values, thoughts, ideas, and my daily actions. I believe in the best that I can become.
26. I am what God says about me, the head and not the tail. I am living my life in abundance not lack. I have more than enough to supply all my needs according to God's riches in glory. I am now living in the overflow. I am successful and happy.
27. Today, I know that I can succeed, and I am successful. If there is a challenge in front of me, I know that I will become even more of an overcomer because of it.
28. I take authority over principalities, powers, wicked spirits in high places. They have no right to attach themselves to my life in any way. I

agree with God and he has me hidden in the secret place of the most high.

29. Today, I can give abundantly of my time, resources, energy, and finances to those who need to be set free from lack, fear, doubt, and unbelief. I live my life on purpose.
30. I live today and conduct my daily activities according to your plan and purpose for my life.
31. Don't be afraid, I have redeemed you. I have called your name. You are mine. When you are in over your head, I will be there with you. When you are in rough waters, you will not go down. When you are between a rock and a hard place, it will not be a dead end because I am God, your personal God. (Isaiah 43:1-3)

Chapter 12

Healing Scriptures

The following scriptures have helped my household get healed, stay healed, time and time again. Read them continually to keep your faith for your health and wellness as God promised it to you in his Word.

Take these daily as you would a prescription drug or medicine to maintain daily divine health. You brush your teeth daily, so use that same concept to speak health over your household and your own body. Many times, we let things slip when we are not in pain, do not have any complications or nothing seems to be "bothering" us. Be preventive with this. Do not let it slip. You would not go a day without brushing your teeth; however if you are an adult, I am sure that you have created that habit and have done it literally thousands of times. Do not let the Word become dusty or dormant.

Take these "by mouth" three times a day until faith comes, then once a day to maintain faith. If your circumstances grow worse, or you feel "something coming on," double the dosage.

Exodus 15:26

If you listen, listen obediently to how God tells you to live in his presence, obeying his commandments and keeping all his laws, then I won't strike you with all the diseases that I inflicted on the Egyptians; I am God your healer.

Exodus 23:25-26

But you—you serve your God and he'll bless your food and your water. I'll get rid of the sickness among you; there won't be any miscarriages nor barren women in your land. I'll make sure you live full and complete lives.

Deuteronomy 7:15

And the Lord will protect you from all sickness. He will not let you suffer from the terrible diseases you knew in Egypt, but he will inflict them on all your enemies.

Deuteronomy 28:1-2

If you listen obediently to the Voice of God, your God, and heartily obey all his commandments that I command you today, God your God, will place you on high, high above all the nations of the world. All these blessings will come down on you and spread out beyond you because you have responded to the Voice of God. Your God.

Deuteronomy 30:19

I call Heaven and Earth to witness against you today: I place before you Life and Death, Blessings and Curses. Choose life so that you and your children will live.

Psalm 91:9-10

Because you have made the Lord, who is my refuge, Even the Most High, your dwelling place, no evil shall befall you, nor shall any plague come near your dwelling.

Psalm 103:1-5

O my soul, bless God. From head to toe, I'll bless his holy name. O my soul, bless God, don't forget a single blessing. He forgives your sins—everyone. He heals your diseases—everyone. He redeems you from hell—saves your life. He crowns you with love and mercy—a paradise crown. He wraps you in goodness—beauty eternal. He renews your youth—you're always young in his presence.

Psalm 107:19-21

Then they cried out to the Lord in their trouble, and he saved them out of their distresses. He sent His Word and healed them and delivered them from their destructions. Oh, that men would give thanks to the Lord for His goodness, and for His wonderful works to the children of men.

Psalm 118:17
I shall not die, but live, and declare the works of the Lord.

Proverbs 3:7-8
Do not be wise in your own eyes; fear the Lord and shun evil. This will bring health to your body and nourishment to your bones.

Proverbs 4:20-22
My son, give attention to my words; incline your ear to my sayings. Do not let them depart from your eyes; keep them in the midst of your heart; for they are life to those who find them, and health to all their flesh.

Jeremiah 17:14
Heal me, O Lord, and I shall be healed; save me, and I shall be saved, for you are my praise.

Jeremiah 30:17
For I will restore health to you and heal you of your wounds.

Joel 3:10
...Let the weak say, "I am strong."

Matthew 8:17
This fulfilled the Word of the Lord through the prophet Isaiah, who said, "He took our sicknesses and removed our diseases."

Matthew 18:18

Assuredly, I say to you, whatever you bind on earth will be bound in heaven, and whatever you loose on earth will be loosed in heaven.

Matthew 21:22

And whatever things you ask in prayer, believing, you will receive.

Mark 9:23

Jesus said, "If you can believe, all things are possible to him who believes."

Mark 10:27

With men it is impossible, but not with God; for with God all things are possible.

Mark 11:22-24

Have faith in God, for assuredly I say to you, whoever says to this mountain, "be removed and be cast into the sea, and does not doubt in his heart, but believes that those things he says will be done, he will have whatever he says. Therefore, I say to you, whatever things you ask when you pray, believe that you receive them, and you will have them.

Mark 16:18

They will lay hands on the sick and make them well.

Luke 6:19

Everyone was trying to touch him, so much energy surging from him, so many people healed.

Luke 9:2

He commissioned them to preach the news of God's kingdom and heal the sick.

Acts 10:38

He went through the country helping people and healing everyone who was beaten down by the devil. He was able to do all this because God was with him.

(God lives and dwells in me, he is in my house and I am healed).

Romans 4:17

I serve a God who gives life to the dead and calls those things which do not exist as though they did.

Romans 8: 2

For the law of the Spirit of life in Christ Jesus has made me free from the law of sin and death.

Romans 8:11

But if the Spirit of Him who raised Jesus from the dead will also give life to your mortal bodies through His Spirit who dwells in you.

2 Corinthians 4:18

While we do not look at the things which are seen, but

at the things which are not seen. For the things which are seen are temporary, but the things which are not seen are eternal.

2 Corinthians 10: 3-6

The world is unprincipled. It's dog-eat-dog out there. The world does not fight fair. But we do not live or fight our battles that way-never have and never will. The tools of our trade aren't for marketing or manipulation, but they are for demolishing that entire massively corrupt culture. We use our powerful God tools for smashing warped philosophies, tearing down barriers erected against the truth of God, fitting every loose thought and emotion and impulse into the structure of life shaped by Christ. Our tools are ready at hand for clearing the ground of every obstruction and building lives of obedience into maturity.

Ephesians 6:10-17

God is strong, and he wants you strong. So, take everything the Master has set out for you, well-made weapons of the best materials. And put them to use so you will be able to stand up to everything the devil throws your way. This is for keeps, a life-or-death fight to the finish against the devil and all his angels. Be prepared. You're up against far more than you can handle on your own. Take all the help you can get, every weapon God has issued, so that when it's all over but the shouting you'll still be on your feet. Truth, righteousness, peace, faith, and salvation are more than words. Learn how to apply them. You'll need them throughout your life. God's word is an indispensable weapon.

Philippians 2:13
It is God who works in you both to will and to do for His good pleasure.

Philippians 4:6-9
Don't fret or worry. Instead of worrying, pray. Let petitions and praises shape your worries into prayers, letting God know your concerns. Before you know it, a sense of God's wholeness, everything coming together for good, will come and settle you down. It's wonderful what happens when Christ displaces worry at the center of your life. Summing it all up, friends, I'd say you'll do best by filling your minds and meditating on things true, noble, reputable, authentic, compelling, gracious, the best, not the worst; the beautiful, not the ugly; things to praise, not things to curse. Put into practice what you learned from me, what you heard and saw and realized. Do that, and God, who makes everything work together, will work you into his most excellent harmonies.

2 Timothy 1:7

For God has not given us a spirit of fear, but of power and of love and of a sound mind.

Hebrews 10:23

Let's keep a firm grip on the promises that keep us going. He always keeps his word.

Hebrews 10:35-36

Therefore, do not cast away your confidence, which has great reward.

Hebrews 13:8

For Jesus does not change- yesterday, today, tomorrow, he's always totally himself.

James 4:7

So, let God work his will in you. Yell a loud NO to the devil and watch him scamper. Say a quiet YES to God and he'll be there in no time.

James 5: 13-16

Are you hurting? Pray. Do you feel great? Sing. Are you sick? Call the church leaders together to pray and anoint you with oil in the name of the Master. Believing prayer will heal you, and Jesus will put you on your feet. And if you've sinned, you'll be forgive-healed inside and out.

1 Peter 2:24

He used his servant body to carry our sins to the Cross

so we could be rid of sin, free to live the right way. His wounds became your healing.

1 John 3:21-22
No longer accusing or condemning ourselves, we're bold and free before God! We're able to stretch our hands out and receive what we asked for because we're doing what he said, doing what pleases him.

1 John 5: 14-15
How bold and free we then become in his presence, freely asking according to his will, sure that he's listening. And if we're confident that he's listening, we know that what we've asked for is as good as ours.

3 John 2
I pray for good fortune in everything you do, and for your good health, that your everyday affairs prosper, as well as your soul.

Revelation 12:11
They defeated him through the blood of the Lamb, and the bold word of their witness.

I would like to share with you a statement of truth. This will enable you to clear your words that you have spoken in the past, as you have now realized the power and the impact of them. Each day is a new day. I would like to guide you and show you how to begin each day with the right mind set.

STATEMENT OF TRUTH

Based upon Proverbs 4: 20-27:

Heavenly Father, forgive me for talking negatively, for speaking deceitful, careless banter, white lies, and gossip.

In the name of Jesus, I will not be trapped or framed by those things that have come from my mouth. I refuse to express myself with negative or contrary things. In the name of Jesus, every negative thing, every evil communication that has come out of my mouth, I contradict with the word of God.

Thank you, Father, for seeing to it that every negative thing I have spoken has been erased from this moment by the power of your word. I no longer say, "I am scared to death, I am sick, I am in lack, I have fear, I have doubt, I have unbelief, I am not good enough", because all of these are rooted in fear. Fear is of the enemy, and I don't belong to him.

I am a believer, full of faith and life, I am not afraid because you are on my side. What can man do to me? You are for me, who can be against me?

Satan, in the name of Jesus, you will not use anything I have said against me. My slate is clean. Thank you Lord, that it is done. Henceforth, I will not speak Satan's lies, but I will speak forth your truth, your word, and I will live the abundant, victorious life that you have provided for me through Jesus Christ, my Lord. Amen.

About the Author

Sherry Elizabeth Brown presents with heart, vision, and integrity. Her training includes both high level strategies and day-to-day tactics that apply to any organization. Her incredible passion, spirit, and energy make everyone better. Along with her ability to communicate, Sherry encourages listening to make everyone feel capable and confident in who they were created to be; and inspires others to embrace all that life has to offer.

As a speaker, Sherry's unique insights on success, prosperity, leadership, and other business-related topics, has fulfilled her lifelong dream— teaching and training others. She believes the best is yet to come, and we all deserve to rise and soar— achieving all your goals, visions, and dreams.

As an independent health coach, her experience with clients on healthy eating, exercise, lifestyle, self-esteem, health education, and environmental issues is invaluable— showing how they each affect longevity and healthy living.

Amassing over 25 years in customer service and owning 3 businesses with her husband, Sherry's ability to mentor has generated a solid client base. As a stellar speaker and trainer, she continues to grow personally and professionally through hard work, passion, and dedication. As a leader she impacts others with her high energy and enthusiasm for life wherever she goes.

Sherry resides in Ohio with her wonderful husband. They have been married for 25 years and have two grown children. The Brown's enjoy traveling and experiencing all that life has to offer. Sherry has a successful network marketing business; is a motivational speaker and a health coach, with a passion to teach the goodness of life, and that the best is yet to come.

CPSIA information can be obtained
at www.ICGtesting.com
Printed in the USA
BVHW042252080821
613969BV00010B/158

9 781734 621143